Albert Blair

A New Suggestion in Ballot Reform

The Registered Envelope Plan

Albert Blair

A New Suggestion in Ballot Reform
The Registered Envelope Plan

ISBN/EAN: 9783337296544

Printed in Europe, USA, Canada, Australia, Japan

Cover: Foto ©ninafisch / pixelio.de

More available books at **www.hansebooks.com**

A NEW SUGGESTION

IN

BALLOT REFORM.

THE REGISTERED ENVELOPE PLAN.

USE IN PRIMARY ELECTIONS.

BY

ALBERT BLAIR.

St. Louis, Mo., October, 1889.

ST. LOUIS:
NIXON-JONES PRINTING CO.
1889.

A NEW SUGGESTION

IN

BALLOT REFORM.

The elective franchise involves both a duty and a right. A free, intelligent and well meaning performance of that duty by the entire body of electors constitutes the best guarantee of civil liberty and social progress. Since the rise of constitutional governments, it has been deemed by statesmen and publicists a matter of great importance to discover, and by fair experiment to prove, the best method of obtaining from the people individual expressions as to their choice of public servants and policies. From its prevalence in the United States and Europe the method of secret ballot, to wit: the secret deposition of a written or printed ticket, has come to be regarded as the one most practicable. The secrecy confers independence, and the characters on the ballot are supposed best to certify the choice of the voter. So far in these respects no better provisions have been suggested. But passing from these two prime conditions, of independence of the voter and certainty as to his expression, it has been found necessary in every State to provide by enactment a variety of additional restrictions and safeguards. Some of these enactments relate to the qualifications of voters and their certification by registration, so as to prevent voting by non-residents and aliens and to guard against a repetition of votes by any voter at the same election.

It has also been found expedient to divide cities and counties into small districts, and to provide that the electors residing in any such district shall be permitted to vote only within their own district and at some place designated therein. This restriction is intended to secure the surveillance of a man's neighbors as to whether he can rightfully, under the law, cast a ballot. Although this advantage is secured, yet the restriction is attended with certain inconveniences and evils. They will presently be mentioned.

It is commonly provided that the ballot shall be deposited in a closed box in the presence of persons, previously selected from the district who, authorized to judge of the qualifications of the applicant, may permit him to deposit his ballot in the box or may deny that right. These persons are for the occasion styled "Judges of Election." As a rule judges of election are fair-minded men, but are not trained to decide controversies of either law or fact. Four judges are usually appointed, two of whom are to be of one political party and two of the opposite party. In theory the political bias of those of one party will counteract the bias of the other two.

This neutralization of two counter tendencies is not in practice completely realized. Superior experience, natural force of character or sagacity possessed by one judge may make him the prevailing mind in determining most of the questions arising before them. It not infrequently happens that the men selected for judges and considered best qualified to serve, on the morning of election fail to attend, and their places are supplied by a choice from those persons who happen to be present. It is a familiar maneuver in closely contested elections, for partisan workers punctually to be present at the polling place at the opening hour and to take advantage of the failure of a judge selected from the opposite party to appear, and to install one of their own selection in his place. Such selections by by-standers are often accomplished without much regard to form and without inquiry into the qualifications of those participating therein.

The acts of judgment devolving upon judges of election are numerous, diverse, and often of such difficulty as either to produce division among themselves or to subject them to criticism by those who are not satisfied with their decision. In cases where there has been a previous registration of voters and they have been officially supplied with a copy of such registration, so far as it relates to their district, the judges are required to consult such registration list in determining who are entitled to vote. It is often difficult for a judge to accept the fact of registration as conclusive upon the right of one applying to vote, when facts within his own knowledge or the statements of credible persons strongly tend to show that the person offering to vote has no such right. On the other hand, the voter's name may have been, either by accident or by design, omitted from the registry and yet there may be incontestible proof offered that he has a right to vote and has been registered at former elections. To the mind of one judge the fact of citizenship should govern irrespective of the registry, while another judge is disposed to stand upon the letter of the law and to regard registration or non-registration as the conclusive criterion.

Question may also arise as to whether one duly registered, but who no longer resides at the dwelling indicated in the registry, but yet resides in the district, has a right to vote.

A printed ticket, having a caption intended to be misleading, regarding its political tenor, may be presented. The question may be urged upon the judges, under the law

in some States, whether it should not be rejected.   In such
cases there is opportunity for serious error to be committed,
involving controversy, more or less dissatisfaction and some-
times the issue of the election.

Usually also it is the duty of the judges to ascertain the
result of the ballots received by them and to make tally
sheets of the same at the close of the election before quit-
ting the polling place.   In canvassing the ballots one by
one, various questions arise and the judges must adjudge.
The more numerous the questions the greater chances there
are for error.   Two paper ballots are discovered to be
carefully folded together, shall both be rejected or shall the
one bearing a number indorsed thereon, when received, be
admitted as legal?   A ticket is discovered to be the product
of two or more fragments pasted together and the law may
require that each ticket shall be an integral paper.   The
judges must decide upon its admission.   Again there is sure
to arise the perplexity so common as to whether a vote for
J. Smith shall be scheduled as a vote for J. Smith or for
John Smith.   On receiving a ballot a judge omitted to
indorse thereon a serial number as required by law ; may he
afterward make the indorsement so as to legalize the ballot?   Suppose further that the district was formerly a part
of the Second Congressional District, but under a recent
apportionment has become a part of the Ninth Congressional District ; and suppose further that there is a vacancy
to be filled in the Second District as well as a regular election to occur to select a Congressman for the Ninth District.
Should there be cast a vote " For Congress " without
designating the District intended, shall the vote be counted
as proper for either district or shall the meaning be inferred
from the name of the person voted for, such person being
known as a candidate in one of the districts? [1]

[1] State ex rel. Broadhead r. Berg, 76 Mo. 136.

From the foregoing instances it is manifest that the judges of election may have a variety of questions of law or of fact presented to them for decision, either in receiving ballots or in counting them.

In such cases it is not practicable for them to hear arguments, or to institute extended investigation, or to obtain the advice of counsel.

The purely ministerial duties of canvassing ballots, making schedules, ascertaining footings and preserving rejected ballots are not performed ordinarily under the best conditions for securing accuracy. The polling place is generally a second or third rate room, shop or shed and is not likely to be conveniently arranged or adapted for performing clerical work. At the close of a day of unusual confinement, perhaps endured without sufficient light or heat, around crowded tables and subject to frequent interruption by reporters or partisan workers, the business of counting, certifying and preserving the ballots is often imperfectly, if not wrongfully performed.

Other evils attend the present system. Owing to the necessity of voting in the precincts in which they reside, it is most convenient for laborers and business men, whose daily employment is at a considerable distance from their homes, to vote either early in the day as they go to their work, or in the evening on their way homeward. Too often there is a delay in opening the polls. The ballot boxes or the schedules have not come to hand, or there is no writing material, or as more frequently happens, there is a failure of some judge or clerk to be present. Most laboring men cannot afford to wait long for the privilege of voting and too many business men are disinclined to endure the inconvenience of waiting. The result is that some go away without having voted and fail to return. In the evening another sort of obstruction is likely to be experienced. There is a crowd waiting to vote and the slow progress the long file is making deters the impatient or indifferent man from remaining. The necessity, commonly existing in cities, of consulting a registry to find the name of the applicant is a hindrance to a speedy receipt of ballots.

Although the precinct system, conducted by judges resident therein, is intended to prevent false personation, ballot stuffing, repeating, intimidation and other crimes against the elective franchise, yet it is notorious that in some communities and in many of the central precincts of a city, the safeguards heretofore provided often prove ineffectual. At the same time the system is attended with the inconveniences above pointed out, and abounds with numerous opportunities for error. These faults have led to a serious consideration by the writer, as to how the method may be improved or another having fewer evils discovered.

The object of this paper is to suggest a method which may be employed irrespective of the precinct plan and at the same time be attended with greater safeguards and less inconvenience. In proposing a new method it is not contemplated to change or abolish registration, but rather to insist that it shall be made more thorough and be accepted as conclusive. Every citizen should have an opportunity to apply for registration. After such application, the officers having registration in charge, should have sufficient time to revise and verify their lists. Each voter, ascertained to be entitled to vote, should receive some document from the officer certifying to that effect. In case an application for registration is rejected there should be an opportunity for a hearing if the applicant so desires. The failure to obtain, through the mail or otherwise, from the officers of registration, a certificate that he is registered would, of course, constitute notice to every rejected applicant of the decision of the Board against him, whereupon he should have opportunity to have the matter decided before the day of election. It being understood that the possession of a certificate by a voter is conclusive evidence of his right to vote ; there will then be no necessity for precinct judges to pass upon the question of his qualification.

The only question for decision upon the day of election would be the identity of the person presenting a certificate with the person described therein.

As an instrument for certifying that the voter has been duly registered and for supplying means to test his identity, it is proposed that the recorder of voters shall issue to each voter, after having ascertained him to be legally entitled to vote, a *registered envelope.* The envelope is to serve two purposes, to wit : —

First. By means of the descriptive notes indorsed thereon to identify the voter.

Second. For inclosing the ballot.

With the envelope the recorder of votes should also deliver *two counter-part stamps* bearing the same serial number, one of which stamps should be fastened adhesively to the ballot before it is inclosed in the envelope, and the other counter-part stamp should be attached adhesively to the envelope after it has been sealed up. The counter-part stamps will serve to identify the ballot, as the one inclosed in the envelope and the descriptive marks indorsed on the envelope will serve to identify the voter as the person whose name is indorsed thereon. The envelope and stamps are to be printed and issued only by the authority of the city and their manufacture or issue by any unauthorized person should be strictly inhibited by law. The envelope may bear an engraving or design, printed or embossed thereon, which shall serve as an official mark. On its face there may be blanks for the insertion of the number of the ward and of the precinct, also blanks for the name of the voter, his street, street number and for short descriptive notes as to his age, height, weight, color of hair, color of eyes, place of birth and occupation.

Registered envelopes should be issued only after revision of the registration lists. Every voter receiving his appropriate envelope will have the assurance that he is entitled to vote, and that such right will not be challenged.

Any one who has applied for registration and at the expiration of the time prescribed for revision of the lists, fails to receive his envelope, will then know that he cannot without it be permitted to vote; and then will be his opportunity for having the matter duly investigated and determined before the day of election. Possession of an envelope by the person named thereon is conclusive evidence that he is entitled to vote, and there remains nothing for him to do but to establish his identity. In this he will be assisted by the description indorsed on his envelope. The descriptive notes on the envelope will, to a high degree of certainty, identify the rightful bearer of it as the person, who under the name and description indorsed thereon, obtained registration as a resident at the place stated in the list.

The collection of envelopes may be accomplished by placing at numerous and convenient stations in the city iron boxes or other sufficient receptacles, each in charge of two judges, whose duty it shall be to permit all persons presenting envelopes and fulfilling the descriptive notes indorsed thereon, to deposit the same in the box. The judges, however, should have authority to reject a vote, should sufficient doubt as to the identity of the voter arise. If the applicant is denied the right, his envelope should be stamped as rejected, and his recourse or appeal should be to the City Hall, where his application should be entertained and an opportunity for proof given.

It would be expedient to station a sufficient number of boxes in the business and manufacturing centers of the city to accommodate men employed therein. This arrangement would greatly favor those mechanics and business men who cannot conveniently find time to go a considerable distance to vote. In the resident portion of the city the ballot boxes need not be so numerous in proportion to geographical extent.

Once or twice during the day boxes at those stations, where the votes are most numerous, may be taken to the City Hall and others placed in their stead. Of course boxes in transit should be sufficiently locked and guarded.

At the City Hall all boxes are for the first time to be unlocked and opened and the ballots counted. Counting may be begun at least by noon, as a good number of boxes from the central districts may be brought in by that hour. As fast as the boxes are emptied, the envelopes contained therein may be quickly assorted into different lots, according to the ward and precinct numbers shown thereon. The board charged with the duty of ascertaining the returns may have for each ward a corps of trained clerks, who, accustomed to making entries speedily and summations accurately, shall ascertain results for each ward; all done under the supervision of the board and under the best conditions for preventing error or fraud and in strict compliance with the forms of law.

The law counselor of the city should be present ready to give advice upon any points of doubt arising in the course of the count.

It is believed that the arrangement proposed whereby all the ballots are to be opened, assorted and counted and the results tabulated at the City Hall, under the supervision of superior officers and under conditions favoring speed and accuracy and excluding opportunities for fraud or confusion, will turn out to be more speedy, certain and economical than the present one, where the counting is done at the precincts. It is also believed that both the incentives and the opportunities for fraud will be fewer under the new plan than under the present one. Many frauds in elections have been the result of a knowledge or impression founded upon a partial count, that more votes are required to carry the day. An unscrupulous ward worker on learning that in certain precincts his candidate has fallen behind, seeks either by use of "rounders" or ballot stuffers or by resort to a nimble change of figures on the tally sheet to supply the necessary number of votes.

In the system suggested no one outside the City Hall will be able to form a decided opinion as to how the vote is going. Every man's vote is sealed in the envelope and all the envelopes bear a neutral appearance. Neither the persons supervising the receipt of envelopes nor those who transport the boxes will be able to know anything of the political tenor of the envelopes received and transmitted to the returning board. This plan will also diminish in another respect, partisan activity on election days. Under the present system it is common for a partisan judge, during the afternoon of election day quietly to make known to an outside fellow-partisan the names of those members of their party who have not voted. The business of driving in the delinquents is thereafter actively prosecuted. Possibly there is no harm in rallying voters for partisan purposes, but the anxiety of the partisan judge, in case a large number of his party are delinquent, is far from favorable to an impartial exercise of his judicial function.

The use of the counter-part stamps, each bearing the same serial number as a means of identifying a ballot with the one inclosed and deposited by the voter, was suggested by the remarks of Judge Brewer in the case of Hudson v. Solomon, tried in the Supreme Court of Kansas in 1878.

" It is a primary rule of elections that the ballots con-
" stitute the best, the primary evidence of the intention
" and choice of the voter. As between, therefore, the
" ballots themselves and a canvass of the ballots, the

" ballots are controlling. This is, of course, upon the
" supposition that we have before us the very ballots that
" were cast by the voters."

" And this presents the difficult question in this case.
" For under the manner of our election, there is nothing
" upon the face of a ballot to identify it as cast by any
" particular voter or even as actually used at any election.
" Nothing to distinguish one ballot from another or
" those cast by the members of the same party, as no file
" or other mark is made on the canvass or otherwise after
" the election, upon any ballot by which its actual use at
" such election may thereafter be established, and as at any
" election there is always a large surplus of unused ballots
" it is evident that if opportunity were offered, ballots
" might be withdrawn from the box and others substituted
" with but little chance for detection.

" Thus in the case before us, if there was but a single
" officer to elect and but a single name on the ballot, how
" easily could one, having access to the box, throw in
" twenty-three or four additional ballots, and thus bring
" about the very difference that appears before us now.
" And who could thereafter tell which was actually voted
" and which subsequently thrown in. The ballot then,
" upon its face containing no mark of identification, we
" must look *aliunde* for evidence of the identity of those
" offered and counted before us with those actually cast at
" the election."

It is true that in most States the receiving officer is required to indorse on each ballot received a serial number,
which indorsement he usually makes with a lead pencil.
Such a notation, as a mark of identification, is not as effect-
ive and indisputable, particularly to the voter himself, as
will be the counter-part stamp, which he himself will affix,
there being no other stamp like it except the one which he
has affixed to his envelope.

As before stated the descriptive notes indorsed upon the envelope are intended as means of identifying the bearer as the owner of the envelope. When a voter applies for registration, these marks can be ascertained over his own signature, verified in part by inspection and entered of record. When the voter obtains his envelope it will be chiefly his own fault, if the envelope delivered to him is either deficient or incorrect in any such note of description. If so, it will be his privilege to have it corrected before election day. Nor need an officer, receiving envelopes, be limited to the information afforded by the descriptive notes in deciding as to the identity of the applicant. Under the system proposed men can deposit their envelopes at a box situated near their work where it will be practicable for any one however humble or obscure to obtain proof as to his identity. His employer or some other person of reputable standing may vouch for him. It is believed that not many political rogues will attempt false personation under this system. To succeed in a single instance, at one polling place merely, would not pay for the hazard thereby incurred. To try a second time at the same place would certainly increase the liability of being detected. Suppose a political jobber buys or steals a dozen registered envelopes from as many different men, the chances are that in nine out of twelve the descriptive notes would be in several respects so unlike his own corresponding marks that he would hesitate to attempt false personation at nine different voting places. And should he be so reckless as to try it, the chances are that he would be detected at one of them.

A number of the substantial evils and inconveniences attending the present system are exhibited in the following array :—

1. Delay in opening the polls ;

    Under this head the following enumeration.

        a. Delay in opening the room designated.

    b. Tardiness or failure of the appointed judges or clerks to appear.

    c. Delay in obtaining ballot boxes, schedules, table, pen and paper or other necessary appliances.

    d. Swearing in of judges.

2. Hasty, informal or illegal elections to supply vacancies caused by failure of judges to appear.

3. Perplexity as to the limits of the precinct.

4. The intimidation of weak men by political bull-dozers.

5. Ballot stuffing.

6. Repeating.

7. " Switching," that is, pretending to receive, indorse and deposit a ticket, but adroitly depositing a spurious one.

8. Rejection of votes on improper grounds by judges insufficiently versed in the laws relating to qualifications of voters.

9. Controversies and affrays arising from differences upon numerous points likely to arise under the present system, but which under the new system *will not arise at the polling place.*

10. The disinclination of many persons, employed at a considerable distance from the precinct in which they reside, to take the time during election day to go to their proper precincts to vote.

11. The overcrowding of voters at the polls during the closing hours of the day, by which some are deterred by the prospect of delay from remaining to vote.

12. Imparting information by a judge or a clerk to an outside partisan as to what registered persons have not voted.

13. Disclosures by judges and clerks as to how their neighbors voted.

14. The practicability of dishonest judges holding back the

results of the vote in a precinct with a view of changing the same if necessary.

15. The conditions of inconvenience and discomfort under which precinct judges and clerks usually make up their returns.

16. The inexpertness of the average judge and clerk for speedy and accurate work.

All the foregoing evils are practically obviated by the new system.

Not being obliged to deposit his ballot in any particular box, the voter need not tarry at any one place, but may at his convenience resort to another. It will be a matter of no importance so far as the act of depositing the ballot is concerned to know what are the geographical limits of the precinct in which the voter resides.

If the timid voter apprehends the opposition of bullies in a particular neighborhood, he may resort to a place beyond their range.

Ballot stuffing or substitution will no longer be practicable, for " no stuff " except the official envelope will either be received or counted.

No man's vote will be rejected except on the ground of non-identity, and any such rejection at a polling place will not be conclusive. The applicant may at once transfer the issue to the City Hall. There being such redress and opportunity for correction, the likelihood of serious affrays *at the polls* over the rejection of any voter will be very small.

The privilege of voting in the neighborhood of their work will induce most mechanics and business men to perform this important political duty.

Overcrowding in the evening at any box is not likely to occur, provided the officers conducting the election have had, during the day, a sufficient number of boxes, judiciously distributed, stationed for the receipt of ballots.

Disclosures as to how anybody has voted will be impossible except by those employed at the City Hall, and as to those so employed, the interest or motive for disclosures will be reduced to the minimum.

False personation is an evil to be named in addition to those above enumerated as incident to the present system; indeed, in the opinion of some who profess to be familiar with ward politics, it is one of the most common and extensive of crimes against the ballot box. As before stated, it is not difficult for the outside worker to obtain from a fellow-partisan judge or clerk the names of those persons in the precinct on the registered list who have not voted.

If, on inquiry, some who are not well known are ascertained to be absent from the city, or for any other reasons are not likely to attend and vote, it may seem practicable to a zealous but unscrupulous committeeman to find substitutes for the delinquent voters. An applicant, so substituted, by simply announcing his assumed name and address, is often accepted as a matter of course, and permitted to vote. It may be admitted that by the connivance of officers, false personation may be accomplished under any conceivable system. And it may be assumed that in the proposed system there may be as great a per cent. of dishonest persons employed as in the present one. But there will be a difference between the old and the new in the degree of opportunity offered for collusion and pre-arrangement. Under the present system, influencing the selection of judges is important business in partisan scheming. Particular persons, for some days prior to election day, are known to be selected for particular precincts as judges, and those known to be weak and servile may be noted in advance. Under the new system, a judge, to be given charge of a box, need not know prior to the hour of service to what district he is to be assigned nor who is to be his associate in such charge.

2

The opportunity for pre-arranging mischief will, by such an uncertainty, be greatly reduced.

It will be practicable for a voter to prevent use of his envelope by any other than himself. This may be done by selecting before the day of election the polling place to which he is willing to be restricted, and having his envelope stamped as restricted and listed as receivable only at the selected station. *He* will know, but *his envelope will not indicate* where he is to vote, so that possession of such envelope by any other than by the rightful owner will be profitless.

As before stated, the proposed system pre-supposes a registration of voters, which shall be to a reasonable degree correct and complete. Possession of a registered envelope by the person named thereon, will constitute conclusive proof of his right to vote. This imputation of conclusiveness may well arise from considerations of public policy; just as in regard to conclusions attained by courts of justice, we are content to accept them as valid and final.

This added import attaching to the results of registration will greatly enhance the responsibility of the officers having it in charge, and, as usually happens in the exercise of trusts, the sense of duty will be proportioned to the magnitude of the interest committed to the trustee.

Another advantage will supervene. If most of the evils attending elections can be restricted to those incident to false or erroneous registration, then the vigilance not only of officers and public-spirited voters, but partisans as well, will be combined and centered upon matters of registration.

In correcting evils, men accomplish most when the proposed reformatory task lies along a single and distinct line of inquiry and action. A small garrison may successfully defend one or two weak points in a wall, but insecurity on many sides tends to distract and dishearten.

In case a voter should lose his envelope, either by theft,

or misplacement, or otherwise, the office, upon sworn application thereto, might issue to him another; but such second or *alias* envelope should be of a peculiar style and be entitled to displace the lost one, should it turn up among those received on election day ; just as the second of a series of bills of exchange when paid by a bank will exclude the first.

Regarding the expense of the proposed plan of voting there are several reasons for believing it will be as cheap or cheaper than the present one. For the sake of an estimate, the City of St. Louis may be taken into consideration. It is a city of probably 450,000 people. The area included within the municipal limits is exceptionally large in proportion to population ; embracing about sixty-two square miles. It is divided into 152 election precincts. To each precinct for an election there are under the present system assigned four judges and two clerks, making an aggregate force of 912 persons. Under the plan proposed the number of polling places need be no greater. There are within the city 75 public school houses, so situated geographically as to bring one within a practicable distance to every child large enough to attend school. A polling place for every school house would in like manner subserve the convenience of every resident. In addition there should be, perhaps, fifty additional polling places within the business and manufacturing districts.

It would probably be sufficient to place two judges in charge of a box, each being chosen from different political parties. The clerical force would be employed at the City Hall. The Returning Board, in choosing clerical aid, would not be obliged to select distributively from the precincts, but might find experts wherever to be had. The vote of the larger wards might amount to three or four thousand votes. Suppose one counting group to comprise four clerks, one to read, one to tally, and the third and fourth to serve as checks on the first two. It is believed that beginning at noon one such group might accurately schedule and count one hundred votes per hour. Fifty such groups would count 50,000 votes by midnight.

In regard to ballot reform much has been lately written in behalf of the Australian system, and in several States laws embodying its principal features have been either enacted or proposed. The leading provisions are that all tickets shall be printed by the State; that an officer shall attend the polls and supply the voters each with a printed ticket containing the names of all the candidates, and that each voter shall have an opportunity, uninfluenced by the immediate presence of others, to change his ticket to suit his views and to deposit it as a ballot.

These restrictions, it is claimed, will deprive political managers of all pretexts for levying assessments to pay the cost of printing and distributing tickets. And the business of buying votes will be greatly discouraged, for the buyer will have no way of knowing that the seller has complied with the bargain.

The system undoubtedly has merits and may well receive consideration, if not a fair trial. But it does not cure or amend most of the evils above set forth as incident to the present system. It would be quite practicable to supplement the registered envelope plan by combining with it some of the features of the Australian system.

The foregoing plan of conducting elections is submitted as an improvement upon the present one, only after extended inquiry, observation and reflection. Many of the evils enumerated are certified either by personal observation or by the testimony of persons known to be versed in practical politics. Doubtless in numerous details, the scheme would require modification, but the main idea, it is hoped, possesses merit enough to justify a trial of it.

In the realm of organic life the law of natural selection

it is said, is slowing evolving progressive structural changes. In physics a thousand trained investigators assiduously renew and vary experimentation in order to discover new properties, adaptations and powers. Amazing achievements mark their beneficent labors. In our national growth it is a laudable thing that while the spirit of conservatism is sufficiently strong to preclude hasty innovation in matters of government, yet there prevails a wide-spread belief that the best in every respect has not yet been attained. When amelioration seems practicable, the old order is not so sacred as to preclude modification. "The cake of custom" has not yet hardened and our institutions, unlike those of India and China, still possess flexibility of form. Where manifest evils exist, whether moral, political or physical, is it not the duty as well as the privilege of an intelligent community to consider means for their elimination? In regard to many of them it will be a wonder some day that society should have tolerated them so long.

THE REGISTERED ENVELOPE PLAN IN PRIMARY ELECTIONS.

In the foregoing paper the writer discussed at considerable length a number of evils incident to the prevalent system of conducting elections. To obviate these evils he advocated a plan which he styled "The Registered Envelope plan." This contemplates that officers having registration of voters in charge, shall, after due revision of the registry lists, issue to each voter a registered envelope. The envelope is to serve several purposes. It will be a certificate that the person named thereon is entitled to vote. By certain descriptive notes indorsed thereon the identity of the holder with the person named thereon is to be ascertained. It will also serve to inclose the voter's ballot, and being duly sealed insures its secrecy. By means of two counter-part stamps, one to be attached to the ballot inclosed and the other to be attached to the envelope, the identity of the ballot as the one cast by the voter may at any time, if necessary, be established. The plan also contemplates that a voter may cast his ballot at any precinct in the city, and that all envelopes containing ballots shall be transported in locked boxes to the City Hall, where they are to be assorted according to wards, listed, checked and counted. It was demonstrated that a good many inconveniences, errors, delays and frauds are made possible by imposing on precinct judges and clerks duties in respect to receiving and counting ballots which those officers are not as a rule, under the conditions under which they serve, qualified to perform. By the new plan, it is argued, much of the inconvenience will be avoided and the opportunities for error and fraud greatly lessened.

Should the use of the registered envelope for voting purposes be found, on experiment, to be practicable and obviate a sufficient number of evils to make it a popular method, the extension of the plan to primary elections by the great political parties would probably ensue. Indeed, it was a sense of the necessity for some kind of improvement in conducting the elections by which political parties in cities choose their delegates to nominating conventions, and by which they select the members of the Central or Executive committees, that first prompted the writer to seek an improvement in ascertaining the choice of the majority of the party.

The ward mass meeting in practice is anything but a fair deliberative body, and too often it is a shameful farce, attended either with gross fraud or scenes of turbulence. It is well known that the more modest and the larger part of the more intelligent voters of a ward habitually neglect the ward meetings. They either find the situation so uncongenial and their presence and voice so overborne by tumultuous proceedings that they are disgusted with the whole

business and for a time resolve to have no more to do with
ward meetings. The primary election, wherein a ticket is
to be deposited in a ballot box in charge of authorized
judges, and under the control of a Central Committee,
has been adopted in some cities in the hope of giving results
more satisfactory to the rank and file of the political parties: but experience shows that it has all the evils of the
present election methods and fewer of the safeguards.
Whether we have ward mass meetings or ward primary
elections conducted according to the present methods, we
still are under the domination of the Central Committee;
which usually implies a political boss and his unswerving
followers. In nearly every city there is established for each
of the great parties a corps of political workers who aim to
keep themselves in control of the party organization. They
largely determine the constitution of the Central Committee,
the choice of delegates to conventions and the selection
of candidates. This compact, invisible but powerful organization is known as the "machine," and is astonish-
ingly self-perpetuating and re-assertive. It is needless to
say that while some of the members are actuated chiefly by
the love of power, others are coarsely corrupt and easily
purchasable. Appointments to Federal and State offices,
as may well be believed, constitute a considerable resource
for supplying aims and rewards for those powerful organ-
izations in large cities; but municipal patronage or plunder
is the chief aliment from which they derive their vigor.
Their "infloonce" with "His Honor, the Mayor," the
City Council and the heads of Municipal Departments is
not permitted to remain long unasserted. For a valuable consideration it is always open to employment. If you
are in doubt where to find its acknowledged agent, consult
the attorneys of corporations which have obtained valuable
franchises from the city; or see the contractors who have
in charge the improvement of streets or the furnishing of

supplies for public institutions. The value of the municipal patronage of the City of New York is estimated to be ten times greater than that arising from Federal offices in the same city.

In thus invidiously characterizing a corrupt party management it is not intended to declaim against proper party machinery and agency. The writer has had too much observation and interest in partisan affairs to denounce indiscriminately all caucuses, committees of control, and other instrumentalities useful in politics. Their utility, if not necessity in promoting party work, is readily acknowledged. There is room for the officious ward worker and the ambitious political leader, self-seeking though they may be, yet it is wholesome, not only for the party but for the country as well, that when a majority of a party desire either for cause or from caprice to displace any particular combination for the time being installed in the management of their political affairs, there should be a certain and practicable method of doing so. It has been found in repeated instances that the ward meeting or the primary election as conducted in the customary way is ineffectual for such a purpose.

One of the offensive things resulting from the domination of a corrupt machine in city politics is that the upstart candidate, without personal merit or experience, but having, as the saying goes, "a barrel," can rally these "machine workers" to his support, in preference to a competitor, however well qualified, who is unable or unwilling to pay their extravagant assessments.

In case of such a competition the problem with right-minded men is, how can the "boodlers" be defeated; but in many cases, unfortunately, the machine somehow certifies the opposite result; and the unclean candidate and his defiled adherents, insisting that he is the *regular* candidate, would constrain honest men to support him or be denounced

as " bolters " or sore-head factionists. The evil originating
in the wards is propagated like a germ disease, and the in-
fection finally extends to the great national conventions.
Men go as delegates of a State to select a candidate for
the office of President, who, at home, are known to be sub-
servient to the worst elements in municipal politics.   And
further than this, the average congressman elected from a
city district, although much preferring to remain un-
trammeled in respect to conferring favors upon his constit-
uents, is plainly made to understand that he is indebted to
the " machine " for his position, and that he cannot safely
ignore its claims upon him.   The result is that during his
term of service he is afflicted with applications for places
which he cannot at heart indorse, but which he has not the
courage frankly to deny.

It is not pretended that all these evils can be corrected
by the proposed improvement, or by any other change, but
it is believed that they can be greatly lessened.   It is not
practicable to keep a field of corn entirely free from weeds,
but their growth to a mischievous degree can be minimized
by the use of proper machinery applied according to approved methods.

Is it possible to lessen the power of money in politics
and to limit the operations of corrupt combinations organ-
ized for the purpose of controlling the action and choice of
a political party?   The fact upon which we must rely and
which should inspire us to make an effort to find a remedy,
is the fact that in every ward of a city, certainly in the
majority of the wards, *a majority of the voters belonging to
any party would prefer to give their support to men of good
repute rather than to continue as their executive agents an
organization notorious for selfish and corrupt practices.*

It is susceptible of demonstration that the " machine "
men and their adherents are not in the majority.   The
trouble is that the majority, inexcusably it is true, do not

make a sufficient, united and persistent effort to displace
them.   The displacement must take place at the primary
election.   There the mischief begins and at that point must
the remedy be applied ; but too many citizens, worthy
in other respects, customarily fail to attend the primaries.   Reproaching them for this neglect will not cure the
evil.

What is the remedy?   *If they will not go to the primary,
the primary must go to them.*   It is worth while to change
the plan of holding primaries if we can obtain the aid of
these negligent voters in our efforts to improve political
practices.

The use of the registered envelope, it is believed, will
make participation in the primaries so easy that no member
of a political party can have a decent excuse for not taking part therein.

Having dwelt at length upon the necessity for some new
method in ascertaining the will of a political party, it will
now be in order to set forth the plan proposed in detail and
to consider how it can be made a practicable measure.

The first step will be the enactment of a law by the
General Assembly to regulate the proposed method and
prescribe a course by which the law may be adopted and
made applicable to any political party within a limited political district.   Its adoption should be a matter of local
option.   It will hardly be practicable to attempt its adoption throughout a large city at a single movement.

The members of a political party, at least a majority of
them, in any ward of a city, ought to be permitted, upon
taking the requisite steps, to obtain the benefit of the Act.
In case the operation of the new method in any such ward
should prove satisfactory, then other wards might and
probably would in like manner adopt it.

A petition signed and acknowledged by a majority of the
party in the ward who are registered voters, might be ad-

dressed to the State Executive Committee of the party asking the privileges of the Act and setting forth the facts required by the Act to entitle them to have the Act made applicable to them. If the State Executive Committee should find, after due notice and investigation, that the averments of the petition are true, they then should declare the Act extended to such ward, and duly certify the fact of such declaration. Upon the adoption of the law by any party for a particular ward, their State Executive Committee should prescribe a form of envelope for voting purposes for the use of the party permanently in that ward. Next they should appoint from the members of the party in the ward three persons to serve as supervisors of primary elections. The supervisors should be, if possible, independent of all local standing committees of the party. Their terms of office should begin and expire in different years, so that any bias of a factional character, possibly affecting the State committee, would not likely be wholly reproduced in the supervisors. The printing, listing and issue of envelopes to the members of the party in the ward for voting purposes, the collection of envelopes and the counting of ballots, should be performed strictly in the manner required by the Act and under the charge of the supervisors. The members of a party within the ward, who are registered voters, may upon written application become enrolled on a list to be kept by the supervisors; and to all such as are enrolled the supervisors, just before a primary election, shall deliver or transmit envelopes, to each his own proper envelope. Any voter on enrollment or at any subsequent time should have the privilege of directing whether he will call in person for his envelope, or whether he will have the same sent to him by mail, or by some designated agent. In like manner the return of envelopes, sealed and containing ballots, may be by mail or by messenger. The envelopes should have printed or embossed on their outward face a distinctive mark, such as will serve readily to indicate the party, by which, and the ward in which it is to be used. It should also contain spaces, suitably arranged and indicated, for the insertion of the number of the ward, the name and street address of the voter and the precinct in which he resides. And all the envelopes for any primary election in the ward should be numbered in one progressive series and the total number issued and the persons to whom issued should be certified by the supervisors before the day of the election. All their lists and certificates should be open to public inspection. This openness or accessibility to public inspection would probably preclude fictitious applications, as the discovery of any such fiction would at once involve the person presenting the petition. If it should be deemed of sufficient importance to exclude members of other political parties from participating in the election, the law may include a section on that subject. An objection to the issue of an envelope to any one on that ground may be decided in a summary manner by arbitrators selected by the parties to the controversy. The supervisors should at least once in every two years ascertain from the Recorder of Voters whether the names enrolled by them are duly registered. Other provisions for preventing error or fraud may be embodied in the Act.

After the names have been duly exhibited and the list revised by striking out any names found not to be registered, and those successfully challenged as not being identified with the party, the envelopes may be issued to the voters or to their authorized agents. On the day of the primary election the envelopes inclosing the tickets of the voters and properly sealed, may be presented by voters in person or sent in by mail or by their authorized agent. In this way the busy merchant or mechanic, or any other who lacks the time or resolution to go in person to the primary, can send his envelope and have a choice in the selection of delegates and in the choice of the member of the Central Committee selected for that ward. A few public-spirited party workers (and there are always a few such men in every ward) would see to it that the less interested members of their party make application for envelopes and that they make use of them by inclosing a ballot therein and have them transmitted to the supervisors. In each ward there are usually a number of men ambitious to serve the party, who will see to it that petitions are subscribed, envelopes issued and returned. In that way it will be possible to obtain the votes of many who under the present system habitually neglect taking any part in primary elections.

It will not be important, as it is at official elections, for the voter at the primary to appear in person to deposit his envelope. If he incloses his ballot and sends it, it is sufficient. If he carelessly or corruptly gives it to another to use, it is simply, so far as the effect upon the result is concerned, as if he created a proxy. If he is willing to abide by the vote cast by his agent, there is not much reason for others to complain. But there is abundant reason for believing that the men, who usually neglect primaries, are not the men who will sell their votes. The purchasable voters are already abroad in the land. They come out under the present system. It is not likely that in drawing out the stay-at-homes the mercenary votes would be much increased. For the purpose of primary elections, the recorder of voters would determine who are voters. Arbitrators would determine whether the applicant is a member of the party he professes to support and the responsibility of the agent named in the petition would insure a proper distribution and return of the envelopes. The result would be a large and independent vote under such conditions, and attended with such documentary evidences as to results that it would not be easy for the "machine" to defeat the will of the majority.

Though not strictly in the line of discussion, it may be permissible in this connection to suggest that, as a means of partially defeating bossism in party politics, it might prove expedient to confer in primary elections the right of cumulative voting. A respectable minority could thereby secure a representation in the delegation of a ward to represent the party at a nominating convention. An alert, intelligent minority, with the courage of decent purposes, may often prevent a nomination, which a less scrupulous but more solid delegation would not hesitate to impose upon the party.

Should the objection be made that such a plan would entail a great deal of work on the Recorder of Voters and on the supervisors, it may be replied that there are plenty of men to be found able and willing to assist in a legitimate work; and there will be no lack of funds to pay for such work if a great public good can be secured thereby. Under the present system immense sums are exacted under the pretense of important party work, and a great part of such money is squandered in corrupt and useless ways.

If there should be the objection that the plan is too intricate, it may be answered that the intricacy is a concern only for the supervisors. Under the directions of the statute, their duties will be no more difficult of comprehension and performance than are those required of Justices of the Peace, Assessors, Assignees, and others whose acts in some measure are prescribed by law. So far as the voter is concerned there is neither intricacy, inconvenience nor elaboration to trouble him in voting under the system proposed. He applies for enrollment, which will be granted to him if he is ascertained to be a registered voter of a ward, and is a member of the party in whose interest the Act has been adopted. He will receive his envelope either my mail, by messenger or in person, as he may have previously directed. Inclosing a ballot and returning the envelope duly sealed to the supervisors, will in like manner be a performance so simple and easy that surely no one would require it to be more so.

The writer appends to this paper a form of a law, embodying such provisions as will, in his opinion, make the measure practicable and successful. No doubt in numerous respects the act as suggested may be improved. But the main idea is earnestly commended to all who are interested in political reform.

AN ACT.

An act to provide a method by which voluntary political associations in certain cases may conduct primary elections.

SECTION 1. The method of conducting primary elections by voluntary political associations, as hereinafter provided, shall be styled the Registered Envelope method and shall become and be binding upon any such association within and for any ward of a city where registration of voters is required by law, whenever a majority of the members of any association, who are qualified voters of such ward and are registered as such, shall, by a compliance with the provisions of this Act, declare their desire to adopt the method herein provided.

SECTION 2. The method herein provided, when adopted by any voluntary political association for any ward of a city where registration of voters is required by law, shall apply to all primary elections thereafter held by such association in such ward, for the selection of delegates to all representative conventions, duly called by the authorized managing committee of such association and in which such ward is entitled to representation; and shall be employed in all elections by the members of such association for such ward for the selection of members of such standing committees, as are by the usages of such association to be chosen wholly or in part by a popular vote of such association within and for such ward.

Section 3. Whenever a majority of the members of any voluntary political association of any ward in any city where registration of voters is required by law, shall, in person, respectively subscribe and acknowledge a petition addressed to the State Executive Committee of such association, declaring that they are respectively residents of such city and ward, are qualified voters thereof and are duly registered as such and stating that they desire to have the provisions of this Act made applicable to such ward, and thereafter to be binding upon such association in conducting its primary elections, and shall accompany such petition with a certificate from the Recorder of Voters, stating that the names on such petition are duly registered as voters of such ward, then such State Executive Committee shall, on receiving from such petitioners the necessary fees therefor, give thirty days public notice in such city that such application has been presented, and shall cause a copy of such petition to be kept for thirty days at some suitable place within said ward, subject to public inspection. At the expiration of said time and after having heard all exceptions or objections to the granting of such petition, said Executive Committee, if they shall be satisfied that such petition has been signed by a majority of the members of such association in such ward and that the subscribers of such petition are qualified voters of such ward, then said State Executive Committee shall cause a certificate to be made by its chairman and secretary setting forth that a majority of the voters of such ward who are members of such voluntary political association, have by a petition sought to have the provisions of this Act made binding upon such association, and that said Executive

Committee is satisfied that such petition is signed by a majority of the members of such association in such ward, and shall transmit the same to the Secretary of State. The Secretary of State, on being paid a reasonable fee therefor shall file said statement and a copy thereof under the seal of his office shall be filed in the office of the Recorder of Deeds of the city whereof such ward is a part. Any Recorder of Deeds, on receiving such copy and on receiving a proper fee therefor, shall record the same in his office, and on the filing of the same the provisions of this Act shall thereupon be binding upon such association in such ward.

Section 4. It shall be the duty of said State Executive Committee to appoint for such ward three qualified voters, members of such association, who shall be styled Supervisors of Primary Elections. The first three Supervisors shall be appointed respectively for terms of one, two and three years next ensuing, and every appointment thereafter made shall be for the term of three years, except where a vacancy occurs by death, resignation or removal, and in such event a successor shall be appointed by said committee to serve for the unexpired term.

Section 5. Any person who is a member of a standing committee of such association, or who is an officer or employe of the State, or of any municipality thereof, shall be ineligible to serve as such Supervisor, nor shall any one who is a candidate for a public office, or who has publicly announced himself as seeking to be nominated as a candidate for a public office, be eligible to serve as such Supervisor.

Section 6. It shall be the duty of such State Executive Committee, upon the issue by the Secretary of State, of a copy of the certificate hereinbefore mentioned, to prescribe a form of envelope to be used for the purposes of voting by the members of such association in such ward in all elections

to which this Act applies, such envelope to be provided with
an adhesive flap for sealing and to bear upon its face some
peculiar mark or design unlike that of any other envelope,
and to have on its face spaces, duly arranged and indicated,
for the insertion of a date, a serial number, the name of
the city and the name or the number of the ward for which
it is intended, and also for the name and address of the
voter, and shall certify the form prescribed to the supervisors of the ward for which such envelope is intended.

SECTION 7. Whenever there shall be called a primary
election to be held in any ward in behalf of a voluntary
political association, which for such ward shall have adopted
the method provided in this act, and it shall be the purpose
of such primary election to choose delegates to any convention to be held by such association for nominating candidates
for public offices or for selecting members of any of the
standing committees of such association, it shall be the duty
of the supervisors of primary elections appointed in the
interest of such association in such ward, on being supplied
with the cost thereof, to cause to be made and prepared a
sufficient number of envelopes of the form prescribed to
supply each of the members of such association within such
ward at the proposed primary election with one of said
envelopes; all of such envelopes to be numbered progres-
sively in one series and to be held ready for issue at least
fifteen days before the day of the proposed primary election and, having so done, such supervisors shall make report
thereof in writing to the City Central Committee of the city
of which such ward is a part and in such report shall state
the number and kind of envelopes that they have prepared
and have ready for issue.

SECTION 8. The supervisors, ten days prior to every
primary election, shall make or cause to be made a roll of
all the names of all voters in the ward to whom they have
issued envelopes during the three years last past, omitting

therefrom only those known to have ceased to be qualified voters in such ward; and a second roll comprising the names of those voters who are members of such voluntary political association and who shall have made application for envelopes since the last preceding primary election; but, for the purpose of voting at any primary election no new or additional names shall be enrolled later than ten days before the day of the primary election.

SECTION 9. Application for enrollment may be made by any member of such voluntary political association who is a voter in such ward and is registered as such, and every such application or petition shall be written or printed and personally subscribed by the applicant and shall state that the subscriber or subscribers are residents of such ward, are qualified voters thereof, are registered as such, that they reside in the places set opposite their respective names and that they propose to co-operate generally with the party or association in whose behalf the proposed primary election has been called. Any number of members may unite in a single petition or application and may designate one or more persons as their agent or agents to receive their envelopes and to return the same to the supervisors.

SECTION 10. The names enrolled by the supervisors shall, beginning not more than ten days nor less than five days before the day of the primary election, remain for three days at some suitable place in such ward open to public inspection. As to all names enrolled for the first time it shall be the duty of the supervisors to apply to the Recorder of Voters to ascertain what names, if any, on such roll are not registered. And it shall be the duty of such supervisors at least once in every two years and after the Recorder of Voters shall have completed the revision of his registry of voters, to apply to the Recorder of Voters to ascertain what names, if any, on any of the rolls by them made and preserved are not registered, and it shall be the duty of the Recorder of Voters, on being paid a proper fee therefor, forthwith to make a careful examination of such lists as such supervisors shall from time to time submit to him, and ascertain by reference to the records in his office what names on such lists are registered voters and what names are not and to certify those not registered to the supervisors.

SECTION 11. Any objection made in writing and signed by two qualified voters and filed with the supervisors not later than five days before the day of the primary election opposing the issue of an envelope to any applicant therefor, on the ground that such applicant is not a member of such association, shall be cause for withholding an envelope from such applicant until the validity of such objection is determined. The issue raised by any such objection shall be forthwith transferred by the supervisors to a committee of three arbitrators, one to be chosen by the objector, one by the applicant and the third by the two arbitrators so chosen ; and the decision of a majority of such committee shall be conclusive of the issue thus brought before them. In case such committee fail to hear and decide such issue before the second day prior to the day of the primary election, it shall be the duty of the supervisors, if requested thereto by the applicant, to appoint a new committee and refer the matter in controversy to them for decision.

SECTION 12. It shall be the duty of the supervisors five days before the day of the primary election to issue to every member of such association who is a voter in such ward and is registered as such and who has previously made due application therefor and against whom no objections have been filed, one of such envelopes, and it shall be their duty to issue envelopes to those in whose favor all objections made thereto have been duly investigated and overruled as soon as such opposition in each instance has been concluded.

And every issue may be either to the applicant in person or to the agent whom he in his application may have designated or in those cases where voters have previously so directed by an order in writing and have prepaid to the supervisors the cost thereof envelopes suitably inclosed and sealed may be delivered by mail.

SECTION 13. The supervisors in inclosing, sealing and depositing envelopes in the mail to be delivered to voters shall do so in the presence of a notary public, who upon the performance of such duty by the supervisors shall administer to them an oath that they have faithfully transmitted by mail one of such envelopes to each voter entitled under this act to receive the same; and such oaths shall be certified by such notary public upon a list of the names of all persons to whom such envelopes were duly posted for transmission by mail by such supervisors, and such list shall be kept by such supervisors, but subject to public inspection.

SECTION 14. At six o'clock p. m. on the day preceding the primary election issue of envelopes for such election shall cease; and no additional or duplicate envelopes for such election shall be issued nor shall such envelopes be issued in any other manner nor to any other persons than provided in this act. The supervisors shall make a list of all the names of voters to whom envelopes are issued, placing opposite each name the serial number of the envelope issued to such person; and the supervisors shall make a report in writing to the City Executive Committee setting forth the number of envelopes issued by them for such primary election.

SECTION 15. On the day of the primary election the supervisors shall receive from the voters of such ward to whom they have issued envelopes all such envelopes duly sealed which such voters may in person, by mail or by their designated agents deliver.

Section 16. In the use of such envelopes for the purpose of voting every member of such voluntary association who is a voter of such ward and to whom the supervisors of such association for such ward have issued an envelope may inclose his ballot in the envelope so issued to him and it shall be the duty of the supervisors to receive the same, but no such voter shall be permitted to use the envelope issued to any other person. It shall be the privilege of such voter in inclosing his ballot in such envelope to indorse or note on such ballot the serial number which his envelope bears.

Section 17. At seven o'clock p. m. of the day of the primary election the receipt of envelopes by the supervisors shall cease and thereupon before opening such envelopes the supervisors shall ascertain the total number of envelopes received and publicly announce such result. The supervisors shall thereupon open the envelopes, canvass the ballots cast therein, and make a schedule of the results of such election and certify the same to the person or persons elected at such election and to the City Central Committee of such association. In case any envelope shall be found to contain more than one ticket or ballot, all of such tickets or ballots so contained shall be rejected and a report thereof made to the person in whose name such ballots were cast and also a report of the same to the City Central Committee.

Section 18. It shall be the duty of the supervisors safely to preserve all envelopes and ballots received by them from voters at any primary election until the time of service for which the persons elected at such election were chosen shall expire.

Section 19. It shall be unlawful for any person without the authority of such supervisors to make or cause to be made envelopes resembling in appearance those prescribed for the use of such association in such ward; and it shall be unlawful for any person to use for the purpose of voting an envelope issued to any other person than to himself; and any person convicted of such illegal manufacture or use shall be punished by a fine of not less than $100.

SECTION 20. Any voluntary political association which may have adopted the provisions of this Act for any ward may repeal the same and become and be no longer bound thereby by causing a petition to that effect to be subscribed and acknowledged by a majority of the members of such association who are voters in such ward, are registered as such and by addressing such petition to the State Executive Committee of such association. In examining such petition and deciding upon the correctness of the representations thereof such State Executive Committee shall give the same publicity and require like evidence as to the facts stated therein as it is required to do in deciding applications made under section three of this Act. If such petition for repeal is found to be true and if approved by such State Executive Committee it shall cause a certificate to that effect to be filed with the Secretary of State and a like certificate to be filed with the Recorder of Deeds in the city where such ward is situated; and thereupon such association in such ward shall be no longer bound by the provisions of this Act.

NOTE. — In the hope of eliciting expressions of opinion as to the practicability of the plan suggested, copies of this pamphlet, to a limited extent, will be distributed to persons familiar with political affairs.

Any communication touching the subjects discussed, whether in criticism, amendment or approbation, will be duly appreciated by the writer.

ALBERT BLAIR.

506 OLIVE STREET, ST. LOUIS, MO.